under a wanton magnolia

poems

maggie stetler

Finishing Line Press
Georgetown, Kentucky

under a wanton magnolia

*For my father and for my mother who, one night in New Orleans,
seeded in me the gifts of art and poetry*

ACKNOWLEDGMENTS

The Small Pond Magazine of Literature: "To Bind a Wound"
The Sow's Ear Poetry Review: "The Room"
Pearl: "Woman of Myriad Seeds"
WomanChild: "Ode: Avocado"
Source, (Queens Council on the Arts): "Constructing a Finite Poem,"
    "Replies to Account Inquiries for Chase Manhattan Bank"
Stone Highway Review: "Body Parts"
The West Wind Review: "love is a vampire," "How to Read a Poem"
Telephone #14 (St. Mark's Poetry Project): "In Answer to Nicole's Poem"
Buddhist Poetry Review: "Spring Journal & Calendar of Days,"
    "Eight Ways of Looking at a Yellow Chrysanthemum," "Bardo"
Snapdragon: A Journal of Art & Healing: "Healing"
Undertow Tanka: "That One"
*Autumn Sky Poetry Daily: "*Anniversary"
Friends Journal: "Surrender"
Anthologies:
Gathered: Contemporary Quaker Poets (Sundress Publications):
    "To Bind a Wound"
Waves: A Confluence of Women's Voices (A Room of Her Own Foundation):
    "What Remains," "Body Parts," "Woman of Myriad Seeds"

Publisher: Leah Maines
Editor: Christen Kincaid
Cover Art: Margaret Stetler & Peter Stetler
Author Photo: Kristin Camitta Zimet
Cover Design: Elizabeth Maines McCleavy

Order online: www.finishinglinepress.com
          also available on amazon.com

Author inquiries and mail orders:
Finishing Line Press
P. O. Box 1626
Georgetown, Kentucky 40324
U. S. A.

Table of Contents

I. lady chatterley & real baby doll

To Bind a Wound...1
The Room 2
A Picture Poem Ending With
 a Line by Pablo Neruda..3
Latchkey..4
Girl with Dolls 6
Knots in a Chain...8
Letter to a Wounded Friend...10
Woman of Myriad Seeds 11
Ode: Avocado...13

II. singing on a broken branch

i never wrote a love poem..17
Father Incantation I..18
Father Incantation II...20
Body Parts 22
Fives..23
Hurt...24
one may morning 26
love is a vampire 27
Mid-Life Cycle 29
Hampton Bays..30

III. a wild chaotic beauty

Constructing a Finite Poem 37
Spring Journal and Calendar of Days 38
Replies to Account Inquiries
 for Chase Manhattan Bank 41
How to Read a Poem..42
Modigliani in Steamy's Café Bathroom 43
In Answer to Nicole's Poem 44
Van Gogh & Vertigo..45
My Mother Sees Into Landscapes...................................46

IV. awake, stunned by stars

Healing..51
What Remains...52
Eight Ways of Looking at a Yellow
        Chrysanthemum...54
Camera Obscura...56
Dance Therapy...57
That One (tanka sequence) 58
Cousins 60
Anniversary...62
Her Garden...63
Last Peach...64
Bardo 65
Surrender..67

lady chatterley & real baby doll

TO BIND A WOUND

She undressed me.
Unwound the wound

behind the question.
I was displayed.

My nudity was white,
malleable, mutable.

Now when I ask
I am a lump of clay

or metal melted down
to amorphousness.

Amoebalike, hands
pray for structure

work the wheel, wield
the clay that is a purpose,

the shape behind the shape
that is my hand.

I build breasts and thighs
of a woman,

a form that moves with mind
to bind a wound.

A wound dressed with a question,
made whole by decision:
                              seize love.

THE ROOM

We slept in twin beds,
wore mother-and-daughter
pleated skirts and blazers
that hung in the green
cardboard wardrobe;
listened to her music:
Frankie Laine, Johnny Ray,
the McGuire sisters. I read
the condensed version of
Hawaii; found *Lady Chatterley*
and the word m-a-s-t-u-r-,
and told her "that's what I do!"
I prayed to my blue plastic
Virgin on the mantel, filled
paper cups with wild red
roses, gave Holy Communion
to my grandmother's cats.
I forgot how we came there
or why, who we left behind
or the addresses of all
the rooms that came after.
But I can smell the close night
air through that window, see
the haloed streetlight, hear
the sudden click-clack of a car
moving toward the avenue.
And I still sing the radio's
wake-up song: from the Land
of the Free, this is Washington's
Double-u, Double-u, Dee-Cee;
may your skies today all
be sunny and blue; W-W-D-C
says good morning, good
morning—to you

A PICTURE POEM Ending With a Line by Pablo Neruda

M

You undid your blouse more like a whore.
I sucked but there was no milk to spare.
Still, you demanded your payment.

O

You shut me out, a colt with no corral.
I ran wild with animal feelings. You knew
how to break me. Even now I cannot find a mate.

T

You knew how to make yourself center of attention.
Arms held high, you bowed to your audience.
I could grab onto an arm and dangle like a monkey.
But if I looked into your eyes, I could not see my face.

H

We were opposites that attracted each other.
I was attached to your strength. It kept me
from flying away. You clung to my sweetness.
It equalized your hidden, bitter dreams.

E

You hid the other half of words from me. You said what to do.
But I heard what was missing. So I was always looking for you.
You handed down a legacy in invisible ink.

R

I dreamed your arm was grafted to my body.
It was acting like you would. I ripped it off and bloodied
my dress. I don't believe what you said: *You will always
be dead or a shadow if you go through life without me.*

LATCHKEY

I walk the mile from school,
wet my pants before I can open
the door. Only Real Baby Doll
who sucks her thumb and cries
when I squeeze her

is waiting. We watch cartoons
and Howdy Doody on the black
and white TV; play with the ones
who live upstairs in shoeboxes
and green plywood

houses. Each day I ask, *How are
you? Oh, I feel sick; I'm afraid
of the dark; I want to go out and play.*
Raggedy Ann never says a word.
When the bombs fall (and

we never know when they may),
I hurry to fix broken arms and legs;
reconstruct fallen walls. At night,
under covers, I do that funny thing;
see swirly shapes on the wall

where the Schmoo clock tick-tocks.
I show Dress-up Girl how to do it; she
doesn't like it at all. After a time, we stop
watching Howdy because Mr. Bluster
scares me. Raggedy Ann tells

stories about a man who visits Mommy
when Daddy is away. The Czech
costume doll wants to know if she's
done something wrong. And Tiny Tears
cries, *It's my fault!*

In the bathtub, I rub hard down there
and see a drop of blood. When I hug
Real Baby, she looks fat and ugly
and old and someone has bitten
off her right thumb.

GIRL WITH DOLLS

Serene, open-in-this-moment little girl, I'm so glad I found you
in this family photo album that arrived by mail. You and your dolls.
You photographed them everywhere. On the steps of Grandmother's
boardinghouse, you posed Dress-up Doll in profile like a fashion
model. With your Brownie Camera, you snapped her, standing full
height like a real person, in front of the Washington Monument.
You captured Tiny Tears perched in a tree, and the Newborn One
with Dress-up Doll and Southern Belle, sitting together on the park
bench like a family.

You hold the Newborn One, with her wrinkled, ugly face, (yourself
barely four) like a real baby. Look at her lifelike thumb and fingers,
bonnet, and crocheted blanket. Both of you are smiling and happy,
in the chair with white doilies on it, and white lace curtains behind you.
This one was taken in Pennsylvania, the land of your father, in the house
of your old-maid great aunt with hairs on her chin, and step-grandmother
whose white hair you thought was powdered at the doughnut shop.

Mother and child, you and doll are. But where, little girl, is *your* mother?
Your father?

There is only one photograph with mother, father, girl and doll. It's
the one I saw first, before the others—before Girl with Doll in Front
of the Christmas Tree, Girl with Doll on My Mother's Back Porch,
Girl with Doll at the Airport. It's the one I keep before me on my desk,
the one I'm looking at now.

Seated on my grandmother's porch steps, from left to right there is
Marguerite: looking striking in a dark dress patterned with large, fully
open roses on long stems with eight leaves on each one. Deep-dark
lipstick and nails. An earring like a bud clinging to her ear. A round,
flat hat on the back of her head, with three pointy black feathers
sticking out from the top.

Next to Marguerite: Raggedy Ann looking a little puzzled at having her photograph taken. High, striped socks, a triangular nose, her hair, raggedy (and surely bright red). Her floppy body keeps Marguerite at a safe distance from the child who holds her.

Holding Raggedy Ann is Margaret Ann: her round Buddha face wearing a contented, serious expression; she has on a dark, stylish little-girl coat and hat. I think I see pigtails, one black-and-white saddle shoe sticks out from under her leggings.

Holding Margaret Ann is Woody: Arm and legs of a tall man, a handsome long German face with receding hair (red you can't see), his chin on her little-girl shoulder, his angular face next to the round girl-face, and now I see a puff of a fluffy feather from her hat touching his forehead; cheek-to-cheek the two of them, so close they look like Siamese twins.

It's the only photograph I have of us all together.

It was in the beginning, Before Marguerite walked out of the picture. Before Margaret Ann went with her because she had to. Before Woody tried to find her, tried to bring her back, but never could. Before it all fell apart.

Before the other photographs were taken with the only one who was left, the one who sat still, who heeded the photographer, who never cried except if you squeezed the sound-box inside her, who fell asleep with you under the covers as you drank juice from tiny, paraffin candy-store bottles, shared sugar babies and chocolate silver-wrapped kisses.

KNOTS IN A CHAIN

I

You dream our relationship is a knotted chain.
 I yank the knots out.
 You are amazed it isn't broken.

II

The night we chased the eclipsed moon around the Rotunda,
we were not mother and daughter, but two sisters searching
for our absent father. You knew the exact spot in the sky where
he abandoned us. I kept us going around, afraid he'd disappear
on one side just as we reached the other.

III

Your balcony is green like the one in this photograph, back
when I wore white cotton underpants, bangs brushed sleekly.
Your magic hands grew snake plants and showy petunias then,
too. Now I must learn my own secrets of earth and seed. I sit
beside you angry and glad: I have survived your long drought,
your shadow on my sun.

IV

Your house opens up into a honeycomb of rooms. My husband
and I sleep in separate cells. I fend off your swarm of words.
You want to drown me in your honey. If I'll be your drone, half
my sex, you'll give up half for me.

V

For years I dream I can't make love because you can see through
my bedroom walls. Sometimes it is you sleeping with me. Once
you placed your wet mouth on mine, pinned me down with your
razor-sharp nails. Now you knock, pitifully, at my door, an old hag
cutting green beans with a dull kitchen knife. I slam the door in your
face and turn to my husband, a wrinkled old man, cheating on his wife.

VI

I go back to 1927 when you were born, hold you in my arms.
You are not the fifteenth child. Your father does not die when
you grow breasts. You do not have a child when you are a child,
or stand between that child and her father. When I am born, you
will be a mirror to me. I will stay safe, grow free.

VII

We wake today, two women eclipsed by love, in need of nurturing.
Knots are yanked free. At forty-three, I realize we are separate bodies.
I feed you fudge and see how hungry you are, buy you gifts, and know
all you've given away. I teach you yoga: On your head with hips and
bent legs in air, you look like a girl. I see how fragile you are, how
strong I am. I see you in me.

VIII

We face each other to say goodbye. I lower a bucket into a well and bring
up my words: *I never give you anything!* Your words stay like stones at
the bottom. A deaf-mute, hands say you. Slowly, fingers spread, elbows
high like wings, fingertips pressed to heart, you say: *Oh, yes, you do, you
give me feelings!* Unused to touch, our arms embrace us and we rock
and weep, rock and weep in our shaped-alike women's bodies.

LETTER TO A WOUNDED FRIEND

Purple grape hyacinths jut up from dark earth, slender penises.
Broken, odd-shaped, multi-colored chunks of concrete placed
decoratively on suburban porch steps (extinct mammals'
footprints, an armed Neanderthal man, a woman entering a cave).

A seven-year-old girl kneels next to her mother on the seat of a
subway car. Gently she bends, places her head in the woman's lap.
A girl becomes a lover, some do not, who have no mother to fling
themselves against, to cling to.

My orange cat sits on my chest. I press my fist against his forehead.
I am a wall he leans into, nearly falls off, falling asleep. Like a lover,
I learn what he likes best as I touch his long, sick, bony body.
Beneath his chin, he loves that one spot.

On the phone, your mother chastises. You're so crazy you
don't know your father when he visits the hospital. I see your
tight-lipped response, behind-glasses glare, a mirror of myself
surrounded, cut off, a scorched tree burning at its core.

I see a man: He saps your strength, ugly, bat-winged, a gargoyle
clinging to your underside. You, poised atop a building, wait to fall,
to shake him off your soft body.

Moving too slowly, missing stride, you mark hours where rest
is required, survey places you now refuse to go and let the words
fall out: "Enough!" and "No!"

In your last letter, before you sign your name, you declare:

> *The earth is dying.*
> *I am trying to save it.*

WOMAN OF MYRIAD SEEDS

She has seeds she has given away
    that are worth nothing.
She says they are wild and rare.
She has seeds and doesn't know
    what flower they came from.
She says they are exotic seeds.
She has seeds she wanted to plant,
    but didn't.
She has seeds she planted
    that shed their skins
    and rotted underground.
She has seeds so tiny, they slip
    through her fingers before
    she can plant them.
She has seeds so tough,
    they can't open out of themselves.
She has white seeds her mother gave her
    that are really salt.
Her mother said they would yield
    a salve for wounds.
She has black seeds her father gave her
    that are hard tacks.
He said it was better to hold a life together
    than to grow.
She gave her daughter seeds that split open
    and grew in air.
She gave her son seeds he spilled
    on the ground.
They grew into two thorn bushes
    she could not tend.
She gave her husband seeds that looked
    like pearls to pay the rent.
He planted them by the roadside
    where they came up weeds.
She gave him the seeds of the weeds
    to pay the rent.

She has seeds that are small and round
      and shiny, and inside them are more seeds,
      and inside them, more seeds.
She has one lopsided seed she has carried
      in her apron pocket for forty years.
It is waiting to grow
                into her life.

ODE: AVOCADO

avocado,
you lushed up
no frail pale lady
you
my own seed
you grew
oversexed
your leaves fat hands
your shoot shooting
no holds barred
you bathed
sun lade
you craved
i saw your size
rise: tits, hips
not my measure
avocado
who knew
i'd love you
sexy queen
green hotbox
my mother
you
I grew

singing on a broken branch

i never wrote a love poem

until a fierce wind battered my heart

until my heart climbed out on a branch

until the branch bloomed then broke

until blackbirds sang on the broken branch

until the river swelled and the tree held its ground

until everyone gathered around eternity

FATHER INCANTATION I

1

I spent the day sealed in a cocoon.
No one entered when I woke up.
I dreamed of a missing man.
Will I keep sleeping?

2

Yesterday I thought: I will never be happy
until I return to him.

3

I am sleeping.
Hot blush on my cheek I seek my father.
Is he limited to one ear?
Is it sleeping?
Can it be whispered to on his pillow?
What does the whisper say?

4

It says: I am here.
I have brought two lovebirds.
I am pigtailed.
I wear yellow muslin.
How far away are you, father?
What shape is your body?
What color are your dreams?
What to you is a daughter?

5

And he   who is he   hushed on the other pillow?
My other lover.
He never measures up.

6

And I?
I am the chieftain's child   blonde and braided.
The sign of the bird protects me.
I wear its symbol in my hair.
Still my finger will be pricked.
Still they will cut off my hair.
Still I will whisper in the shell of my father's sleeping ear:
Where? Where? Where?

FATHER INCANTATION II

1

She mourns today.
Last night the dream came back.
Crazy Horse died.
He fell in his golden-feathered pride.
His bride-to-be watched and wept.
And part of her died.

2

Who's calling?
Is it you father   in the marigolds?
Is it you father   gold in the road?
I hunted you   monkey gold   was I fooled?
Did you die?

3

In my dream you and I left in a black hearse.
There was a bride and groom inside.
After the divorce I wished you dead.
You died.
Otherwise it was too real.
Saying goodbye   never seeing you again   knowing
You were still alive.

4

But last night the dream came back,
And I need to know:
Which part of me are you?
Are you my bound heart?
My closed ears?
My lower half that lies in the ground?
Did you plant me, waist up, a pretty face?
Waist down, twisted?

5

Show your face father   let me claim you.
You are my roots.
Say you're not the bald sky.
Say you're not the bald eagle's bright lidless eye.
Father my fire goes out   dead smoke   calling you.

6

It was nineteen years ago.
Today I try to phone you.
You have children   a wife.
Not me   not mother.
You are fifty-four years old.
Do you still grow the gold marigolds?

7

I have grown.
You may not like me.
I'm not an Indian princess.
I live with another man.
When you left I was only eight.
I would masturbate.
I thought you would marry me.

8

Come back!
When will you spring from my side
Alive?

BODY PARTS

Leg lies on the rug like a dog's gnawed bone.
Arm against the bookcase.
Foot in its slipper beside the chair.
Under table glass, head with blood-matted hair.

The house is dark, vulnerable to sky and earth
the way the sleeper is to wakeful, watching ones.

In the dream I ride with a stunt driver, a man I love.
He speeds to the edge of a cliff, has seconds to brake.
I count on him, he fails, the car flies forward into air.
Down in the mall, shoppers pick through the pieces.

A murderer is still in the house.
Let me reconstruct the crime:

I rise up tall and proud in my young body.
Each part belongs: arms, legs, hips, belly, thighs, head
and moves as a whole.
Even my breasts, too large, surely not mine, are lovely.

I leap, turn, lift arm and leg in arabesque.
The intruder raises his arm.

I am not dead.
I still have my best parts: my voice, my sex, my heart.
Only I cannot carry them on legs, reach out with hands
or hold with arms, my self or another.

I cannot see who remains in the dark.
But I know he is weeping.

FIVES

—Inspired by Philip Dacey and Frederick García Lorca

Fingernail moon hangs in the sky.
The night, dead and deep.
Snow quiets, keeps us safe.
You whisper to me under covers.
It's the fifth week of the new decade.

Safely you walk towards me in your rose-grey body.
I count five: two arms, two legs, a head.
I measure your penis with my smooth gliding.
Ice-sailing over glass that rings.
I met you when ice broke with spring coming.

I lie because it's night and all but a slice of moon missing.
It was summer past the fifth month of yellow moons.
On the park bench, your leg in loose pants, my bare knee.
I said my Rosary as a girl and honored a statue with roses.
You broke through the underbrush and flushed me out.

At five I loved a boy on a mat at naptime.
I told only you all my story to keep safe.
The trunk of the magnolia split in two then bent toward itself.
We loved on a braided rug, hard and deep.
As a child, I fingered my sex, feigned dying.

Five in the morning begins a journey.
Our child would have been born after such a cold night.
An ice floe breaking off from his mother.
You have sealed your eyes and ears against the wind.
Walk with me, the light tells its own direction.

HURT

you are so
beautiful

it hurts

to look
at you

i hope no
one gets

hurt
she said

i hurt
you

you
hurt
me

we
hurt
so many
times

comes
a time
when
all that
hurt

curls
up
into
a tight
ball

into
the
tiny
flailing
fist

of a
hungry
baby

and all
we can
do is

pick her
up and
hold him

we recog-
nize our-
selves

we are
so

hurt

and
so

beautiful

one may morning

oh this morning is a
wild one
i repotted the geranium
one living marigold died
we walked in the garden
you stark   dark
myself an empty rain barrel
we talked about the marigold
which one killed it
you with your overdose
me with lack of care

oh this morning is a wild one
i am close to earth in overalls
looking for the magic words
seeds i can't find
the cat dug up
i planted wrong
RAIN you say   NO
just as well they die

this morning is wild
why
it looked like rain but didn't
also
we didn't decide who
satisfied it died
we kept walking
stopping where the earth
was warm   firm
we took in the morning
without trying to change it

love is a vampire

but sweet,
more entertaining
juicier
like sucking on a thousand
pomegranate seeds
one at a time

coming on
an apple orchard in bloom
with the moon up
at midnight

reading a John Donne poem
in the bathtub
by the light of
a candelabra

or remembering Marilyn Monroe
in that photo
her dress spiraling
over her head
shocking pink panties

and of course, tongues
of iguanas, don juans
red felt ones
on Teddy Bears

and lips
(not to forget the teeth)
INCISORS

ah, vampires
the lust of just one
sexy night stalker
dressed in his long black cape

your window open
a convincing scream
a helpless faint

and then, afterwards
the two of you
holding hands

watching the end of the late show
before he goes back to work

MID-LIFE CYCLE

Full moon at mid-month.
His hand circles her milk-white breast.
In the garden a birdbath drinks the moon's light.
She looks in her mirror, sees the moon.
He kneads her belly and wants a child.

A cloud crosses the moon, darkens it.
She brushes away hair fallen in her eyes.
He looks into her eyes, sees the cloud crossing.
She closes her eyes and dreams
Of a tiny moon rising in her body.

It bends on a slender stalk, opalescent moonflower.
Wafer-thin it will burst and bleed on the wane.
Washing away life, it will ride through her.
Unless his stickiness sticks.
Then no new moon for nine months.

Instead a mushmelon will grow, a sea creature.
All eyes and head, its lifeline tied to her.
She imagines her belly balloon, a smaller balloon inside.
No more gazing-at-the-moon moonlit evenings.
Only the creature's underwater tossing and breathing.

Now the bleeding.
It leaks out like a deep cut or bloody nose.
How many moons are left? he wants to know.
The moon swelled in her grandmother sixteen times.
She gives birth in a dream to a jellyfish that feeds on her.

Now the mirror reflects only her moon face.
Little fish swim backwards inside her.
The moon is a dish run away with the spoon.
Night takes a bite of the moon,
Dims its white light. Still, the moon rises.

HAMPTON BAYS

Sun, Air, Night and Moon

1

I wake in the morning, open curtains on three sides. Air, sun,
and green surround us. I watch as Shinnecocks once did,
light filtering down through tall pines.

2

I put on the lilac swimsuit, first one in years. Fearing signs of
middle age, I'm startled by deep cleavage and pelvic bones.

3

Lounging on the deck, one hand on the other sinks into my
belly like a stone. I am dazed, drunk, drugged with air and sun.

4

We go to the beach, not to bathe or sun, but to watch the moon
come up. It grows white, small, as trees along Squire's Bay blacken
into mystery. Purple pierces the distance between the white gull
and black swift.

5

We move the Persian rug, push twin beds together. You fall asleep,
wake in the night, frightened, calling my name.

The Direction of Things

6

You sit fully clothed, an Arab under a rain umbrella. I stay by water's
edge, struck by rock-filled waves. When the wind catches our umbrella,
I am forced to enter the bay, you to look the sun in the eye.

7

We see signs in seaweed trails left at low tide, in delicate etchings
on driftwood, on rocks where time, water and sand have crisscrossed.
God and the sea are talking to us. But what are they saying?

8

On my left, the sun goes down, round and pink. On my right, the moon
rises, grows white. In front of me, the bay at high tide and distant
land. Behind me, backwater and long-legged bitterns. Above, darkening
sky; below, luminous sand.

9

You draw the moon down in a photograph of my round face, paint it stark
white against black trees, then tie it to the earth with a ribbon of purple.

Housekeeping and Night Visitors

10

A spider by the wicker basket has spun a great web. Her prey, five or six
corpses fallen on the floor, lined up at odd angles. I sweep around them.

11

At the local supermarket, we buy chicory coffee, green onions, charlotte
russe, bass ale, a citronella bucket, beans, garlic, and French bread. We
scour antique shops for treasure, return with a chipped blue jar.

12

At midnight, you make *pasta e fagioli.* I go out the front door and
come back in again to savor the smell of cinnamon and sage.

13

The neighbor's cat presents herself upside down. Later, a raccoon peers through the sliding glass. Moths, beetles, daddy-long-legs home in on the porch light, cling to the screen. In my dreams, fantastic wings beat against an invisible pane.

Good Ground

14

An old man fills us in on local history. Rampastures, his home, a night spot that jumped in the 'Twenties. That was seventy years ago, now, his teeth, crooked and yellow as summer corn.

15.

We walk along back streets: The Trail, Newtown, The Canal, Red Creek, Bittersweet Avenue. By a row of fragrant white flowering hedges, you say "Smell," and with a sweep of hands, "Now, THAT'S summer."

16

Bus to Southampton, over hills where Black Indians live. Boutiques and eateries beyond our means, we cross tracks for a luncheonette and grilled cheese. You buy a hat to hide your balding head.

17

After the first sunset at the Vernal Equinox, you remark how "the light rakes across the sky." For a stretch of too many days, the sun is dimmed by low stratus clouds.

18

We break our long vow of celibacy, come to sex as if it was our first
time. We want to prove we can still do it, and of course, it's not how
we remembered.

Ghosts & Leave-Taking
19

On our last night the sun hangs on the horizon. I name it "egg over
easy." Rays scatter, sink into the bay's Western end. Like the couple
we see in the distance, two grey specks, we walk in shallow pools
left by the outgoing tide.

20

A great grey bittern steps tentatively on slender legs, claims the
backwater of Squire's Pond. Reluctant, we step into the road,
leave darkening beach and bay behind.

21

In my dream, winter piles up snow and dead insects. You are not
there. I wake up longing for what I can't see. All night I wage a war
against long-ago loss and new endings.

22

In morning, ghosts given over, cab called, I run back inside
to collect forgotten shells. I find you *davening* a silent prayer.
Not knowing what lies inland, we close the door.

a wild chaotic beauty

CONSTRUCTING A FINITE POEM

Finely cut, faceted, its shape defined,
simple, altered by bare glass against black sky,
obscured by a sudden floodlight illuminating
a taut, pensive, female form;

Dreaming, rearranging the angular,
disparate parts, composing the stanza of the poem
a man would have written, she would have called
solid shapes, ovular paths, night wind;

Breathing, casting out space, gathering
facets of an abstract movement, perhaps a rite,
it reappears as a meteor, reminding her
of how he almost died;

Piercing the stars, the plot is geometric,
angular, pristine, a crystallization bound by
surfaces, a diamond as cold as stars, as precise
as their definitive, white light:

Constructing this poem, propelled by an
unidentified object, identifying its illusive
form, interpreting its silent name, calculating
its swift departure and return, stopping—

Suddenly, I see myself in a photograph
On my desk:

Young, smiling, in a sunsuit,
a lilt of a girl caught in sunlight
in front of dark shade trees, in love with
summer or some foreign object in the foreground
perhaps a butterfly, perhaps the photographer
perhaps the dazzle of the sun breaking up into fine particles

SPRING JOURNAL AND CALENDAR OF DAYS

March 6. INSECTS AWAKEN (According to the *I Ching Daoist Book of Day*s)

I am inspired to write a poem by words that astonish me:
insects awaken. I never knew they were asleep.

March 9.

My father's spring letter arrives. He tells me the other day
he spied a speck of orange near the backyard shed. When
he focused his binoculars, he saw seven robins. A lucky sign.

March 15. Beware the Ides of March (from *Julius Caesar*)

Our local politician drives a 12-inch kitchen knife through his heart.

March 20.

Hooplah! Verily! Tra-la! And *sing cuccu!*

March 25.

7 am. I lift the dead, packed leaves off the flowerbeds.
7 pm. Line bright-colored Gurney seed packets in rows on
the dining room table and draw a map of this year's garden.

March 30. Easter Sunday

I read in the Sunday paper that Easter is always the first
Sunday after the first Full Moon following the Vernal Equinox.

April 1.

Suddenly, without warning, everything is growing.

April 23. Will Shakespeare's Birthday

We make a Seder and say ancient words: blood, fire, pillars
of smoke and IT HAPPENED AT MIDNIGHT.

April 28. Our Wedding Anniversary

Thinking of our Quebec honeymoon: a cold spring wind blowing
off the St. Lawrence, fragile birds made by nuns in the Old City,
a bedroom behind a red-leather double door.

May 1.

Plant marigolds, zinnias, cosmos, nasturtium, Love-Lies-Bleeding
and moss rose. Hollyhocks, comfrey, Basket-of-Gold and shoots
I can't tell from weeds are already growing.

May 3.

I find, in my house, a pair of birds in a cage. I haven't fed them
for years, yet they're still alive. I find two foxes in a container,
hardly breathing. Other animals: a toad, a mouse, one without
feet, one without a tail. I wake and write about the animal parts
of myself: deformed, stunted, *coming alive....*

May 8.

I let the tomatoes that my neighbor lady grew for me die. After a
brief search, I find new plants in the supermarket and put them
into the ground.

May 26.

My friend throws a party on her fortieth birthday. Friends
give her sexy negligees and a trip to the Poconos. She is
planning to have her first baby.

June 11.

The mimosa tree blossoms, loses all its leaves. It's been
struck by a ground wilt and is dying. The birdhouse
my father built hangs from bare boughs.

June 21.

I throw the *I Ching* coins and the oracle says: Danger comes
from a seed of evil in yourself. You must weed your heart
like a garden, free yourself of encumbrances, and take care
not to destroy vital, new growth. If you are open and yielding,
relationships will flower. It is time to discover yourself.

REPLIES TO ACCOUNT INQUIRIES
FOR CHASE MANHATTAN BANK

Oh to traverse Battery Park
divine the origin of Rector Street
smooth my hand over Alexander Hamilton's grave
(dead at 47 years) and in a revolutionary way

startle the streets with pipes and drums
the varicose dreams that lie beneath
emptying into Walt Whitman's seacoast.
Out of the cradle endlessly rocking

Manahatta, where are your poets now?
Asleep over IBM electrics, they think of how
Joyce rebelled: sneaking in songs of themselves
before the Chinese office girl—dusky, mysterious

like Fedallah in *Moby Dick* (Melville that other poet
stunned by the violet sunset, last night crossing Broadway)
—reappears with a fresh stack of forms to type.
Was it that way, Herman, at the Customs House

(where I read my poems in May), your white whale
in your eye, a stack of official papers under your arm?
Oh to rush out onto Thames Street
stop off at Trinity Church and count the angels

compare them to a Rilkean sonnet or clipper ships
and then lunch anywhere but at the corporate cafeteria
—1 Chase Manhattan Plaza, Nassau Street

HOW TO READ A POEM

For hungry readers: Eat a poem for lunch. Bite into and chew the precise meanings of each word. Savor the tastes and textures: sesame seeds and macadamia nuts (fertile allusions); avocado slices (rich connotations); crispy lettuce (fresh transitions); and green goddess dressing (tangy inspiration). See how it all hangs together in a homogeneous salad-poem. Imbibe the feelings and recall your first meal on warm mother's milk.

For the lazy reader: Sit in the bath and let the words seep into your pores. This is a good way to identify forms. (An ode causes red skin; an elegy, goose bumps; free verse, a floating sensation.)

For more sensuous readers: Take the poem to bed. Hold the metaphor in your arms, caress the images, feel its assonances and judge it by how well it loves you back.

For more spiritual types: Record a dream and type it. Retype the poem you're reading on onionskin. Then place the dream behind the poem, hold both up to the light, and read your dream behind the lines of the poem.

For less confident readers: If you do not understand the poem, select several nouns from the poem that strike you. Then go outside and find the real object in your yard, down the street, or in a nearby park. Stare at it for ten minutes straight: *bucket, worm, dandelion, stone, tarantula.*

For wounded readers: If you still don't understand it, pretend you are a paramedic service. Have a friend call you up on the phone and read the poem to you as if it were an emergency. Respond properly to save its (and your own) life. This works on even the most meditative Oriental forms.

MODIGLIANI IN STEAMY'S CAFÉ BATHROOM

How elongated the plunge of your
   neck, how flushed
your cheeks. Women sit in
envy, their backs to your almond eyes.
Men confront your masklike face

     with a warm outpouring of praise aimed
at your twisted contours. They say
Amedeo may have given away
your original for a bagel
and a latte.

Your narrow nose, your pursed lips
    move many to stay for as long as it takes.
Pale splash of rose and purple flesh
match the décor of lavender soap,
slightly damp floor.

       I am relieved—
    fears of public accidents wiped away
knowing when my poem is written, my
Mocha Monkey Smoothie
downed—If I have to, I can go again—

and more fluid than Picasso's
cubes, more open than Mona
Lisa's smile,
   ac-commod-ating,
        you'll be there.

IN ANSWER TO NICOLE'S POEM

Cul de sac, chemin, toujours Baudelaire, "may he rest in peace," we are waiting
for dinner, *à la Quebec.* She wrote, Nicole, a polite poem translated by the one
who speaks *un "peu"* which the poem was. We are learning French in an instant:
nouveau poésie not pottery; *salade aux oeufs* instead of salmon. The St. Lawrence
spins on top, *côte de montagne. Chambre à louer.* He is painting the Frontenac:
green roof in evening. A woman with crocheted breasts. The *ascenseur.* It is raining.
Persian cats, Pekinese. Kaybek travel fun: *fermez la porte, la toilette.* Pale orange,
I am restless, reeling. Hurtubise discovered! *Le Livre des Heures.* We are carrying
pâtisserie. He is painting the wall of the city (walls around my heart he is painting,
unpainting). Only 3 entrances originally: St. John, St. Louis, Kent. Players he is
smoking. Indian pudding, pea soup, *creton, lait, S.V.P.* We are wearing old clothes,
our hair cut. *Printemps.* Old canadien wine. We are learning French: *La Place Royale,
Hurtubise, Michele Poulin, La Chateau de la Terrasse.* I will take a *bain.* Nicole had
"les Peines." She thanked you in the poem translated by the *amateur.* Dreaming I am
green, too tired to write; a bath is better. In Quebec it is *frawh*(?) but the bath is warm.
Is this *amour?* Pink *negligee* (French), the sex *(femme)*, green the short *negligee,* the
sex is French *à la mode. We are eating a lot. OUI. Cezanne, Matisse,* canadien cheese,
old wine, spirits, *bière.* Only the Yashica is Japanese. *Fleur de lys.* French for travelers:
Parlay-voo-Anglay? "I have heard of Francis Ponge. "Do you like this Argentine print?"
"We are moving to Martinique." "Good luck with your pipe dream!" JUST MARRIED!
Veal marengo, bordeaux, chocolate mousse, asperges vinaigrette. Dostoevsky in French,
"Peanuts" in French, Chinese food in French, a French poodle, Dustin Hoffman
and Steve McQueen, in French. *Merci Beaucoup. Merci. Merci.* Orange cornflowers,
butterscotch drops, Vermeer, *Poésie Quebec, Sucre 81¢.* Painting the *Chateau Frontenac*
green gold at night. *Cul de sac.* Old wine, cheese, bread, eggs, *lait,* freeze-dried Maxim.
The green *negligee. Soleil. Soleil de Quebec.* Thursday night: *Anciens aux Canadiens.*
Outside the walls the city is normal. Like New York City. Pies and tarts cost less. *Ventes.*
Walls and cannons, the mountain, green roofs, red roofs, narrow streets. *BONJOUR!*
Glass windows, leaded, stained, oval. Double doors, steps. *La Place d'Armes.* Pale green,
the walls. *S'il vous plâit,* a poem folded on lined paper, a handmade envelope, paper
clipped, signed Nicole xxx ❀, in the cupboard at the *Maison Acadienne.*

VAN GOGH & VERTIGO

—On Viewing Neena Jhaveri's Free Spirit

I jump into a whirl of tangerine fishes spiraling
in citrine and metallic gold.
An octopus undulates in eggplant and cinnabar.
Smells intoxicate: voodoo lilies, ginger,
passion flower. In a vortex of indigo, I tread tangelo,
surface on rice paper, wet with the sticky flesh
of papayas, avocados.

I put on the painting to get away—a psychedelic scarf,
it trails me, flips the foreground, fuels the turbulence.
I hunt for negative spaces—there are none;
colliding shapes of blellow and octarine pull me
into a cyclone of Van Gogh and vertigo—
and no way out of the bloodlust red.

I birth myself under honeydew breasts, a Siren's
vermillion eye; ghost-white looms but chartreuse gains speed;
spinning past fandango, dizzy with lime—flying, flying—
I gain strength, *figuratively*, run past the periphery, FREE
—does she see, the dark-eyed painter,
brush in hand, laughing?

MY MOTHER SEES INTO LANDSCAPES

I.

My mother sees into
landscapes, out past the
yard, the goat shed, field
and mulberry tree into
purple mountains where
she dabs wildly, tries to
stay within the lines, leaves
a fugitive trail of cobalt blue,
burnt sienna. She flees
interiors, leaves the
foreground undefined,
does not see into what
she sees or who is
waiting. First steps by the
Reflecting Pool, she runs
toward sun, stopped
by shadow: the man
behind the camera.
Now she paints herself
into a corner and the way
out goes dark.

II.

My mother looks past
love and healer's
hands. Chest tight, jaw
set, she breathes past
breathing (lungs in
shadow now). She spies
a warning. *Why?* This
self-portrait: a car, a man,
front seat, a hand, seven
years, over and over left
on a familiar doorstep.

Past that she blots out
home, love, man,
marriage, another man,
marriage, another man.
Tonight, blazing dim, she
cracks dirty jokes, sees
husbands in the Valley Road.
As they lift her gurney above
me, she shouts, *Don't forget
to feed the birds!*

III.

My mother flies past
morphine, machines
and white light, out of the
room before she's gone.
She will not look death
in the eye. Ophelia on
high, she surrenders
in absentia to a rape of
whispers, hands, quarrels,
prayers and a wild chaotic
beauty. *Swing low sweet
chariot*, a man calls the
final tune. Does she see
me cut her hair and cry?
I've painted a picture
of this: A spiral lock of
silver grey, still-alive.
Columbines (lavender),
coreopsis (sun yellow),
on white sheets. A streak
of fire, a smudge of
stardust, *burning*.

awake, stunned by stars

HEALING

If a promise is broken: Get behind the broken words and look
through them as through a broken window. Pick up the pieces
of the promise and rearrange the letters to form new words:
"Rose," "Sperm," "Ripe," "Rise," "Spire." Compose a prayer
with these words and ask that you may become strong.

If a marriage is broken: Let the child of the broken marriage speak.
Let her ask her father: *Do you still love me? Ask her mother: Is it
my fault?* Let her make wild wishes and do not laugh at her: *He
will come back. She does not love another man.* Let the marriage,
not the child, break in two.

If a spirit is broken: Let it ride a great horse through night air, collect
on its coat charges of light, salt crystals, abandoned shells of insects.
Let it enter the other world and receive the name, *Ghostdancer*; and
a black mate of untamed wildness. When the spirit returns, let it be
as charging breath, fire on the tongue, a serpent hissing, uncoiling.

If the body is broken: Carry it to a place in the earth that smells
of must and decay. Lay hands on the broken parts. Speak words
that enter the body. Press the spinal column with two fingers
and say: *Let light enter, dying cells pass out.* Smooth the forehead
and say: *Let air flow into the corners of the eyes, out the top of the head.*
Gently grasp the genitals and say: *Let one enter another, again and again.*

If a life is broken: Study the power of breath. Watch how the living body
breathes in air and breathes out. Consider how your body is not the
first this air has entered, how it has entered and left the bodies of other
persons, wild animals, insects and plants. In the last breath, pass into
breath beyond breath, life before life, the final where of who you are.

WHAT REMAINS

—Remembering Virginia Woolf

I.

As a woman, I guarded
my body too, longed for a
mother, not a man, married
for love and art but not sex.
As a child in Pennsylvania,
I dodged imaginary Cold-War
bombs, pre-divorce barrages.
In London, yours, a real war.
No matter, wounds concur:
woman down. Still you met
head on: fiction, insanity, the
folding over of mind and world.

II.

You, buffeted, frail—your words
shot me out of orbit. A blast of
truth lodged in the central nerve.
A kaleidoscope of self
and others fused, refracted;
time and space collapsed,
colliding. I rode your waves,
voyaged out and back, safe
by your piercing light. For you,
repercussions: headaches,
despair, voices. You died
many times before you died.

III.

I stand in the 21st Century
on my river bank. Cast
a stone, wade out, tread
water, float. Easier than
your walk, still a distance.
Other side, sepia in morning
haze, you wave recognition.
In a second lasting 130 years,
your body bursts into flames.
What remains: a spinning thread
of connection—blood, veins,
hair, gut, gamete—all *pure gold*.

EIGHT WAYS OF LOOKING
AT A YELLOW CHRYSANTHEMUM

1. *Winter Solstice*

Yellow pheasants stop their cries. Tigers start to pair.
In the eleventh month, the chrysanthemum mirrors
the sun's diffuse rays.

2. *According to an 11th Century Japanese Herbal*

Gather the young shoots, flowers, stems and roots at
their peak. Dry and reduce to a fine powder. Take three
times a day for one hundred days. In a year, grey hair
will return to its natural color. In two years, new teeth
will replace those that have been lost. And in five years,
a man of eighty will be a boy again.

3. *Chrysos Anthos: Gold Flower*

Unlike the rose, it smells like an antidote to love.
Unlike hothouse tulips, its petals are fixed as a lion's
mane. Unlike a daisy, the chrysanthemum never
says, "Loves me, loves me not," but chants, "Hold
together" and "Stay."

4. *Sixteen Complete Rays*

The chrysanthemum is a widowed matriarch surrounded
by sixteen devoted children. In life, they crown her and
cling to her. When she dies, they die with her.

5. *A Luscious Drink*

In a rectangular box from Shanghai, little dry, yellow-white
heads. In a brown clay pot, hot brew topped with licorice
bark, gnarled hawthorn and honeysuckle curls. Fan the
spirit-filled steam from cup to nostrils. Sip the citron-colored
liquid. Smell wet wood burning.

6. In the Language of Flowers: Love Slighted

An aging woman sits straight-spined in a ladder-back chair.
In her lap, a poem written by a man. It says: You shattered
my dreams. On the desk, a photograph: the man's face torn
away, only hands hold a girl-child. Bending, the woman
writes: I am more withered than the chrysanthemum's
dried flowers.

7. Pictures of a Floating World

On a courtesan's broad sleeve: crests of waves, billowing clouds,
yellow chrysanthemums. On the center sheet of a triptych, an
actor-peddler carries the Four Seasons on a flower stand: Winter
Plum, Spring Cherry, Summer Peony, Autumn Chrysanthemum.
On a sliding door, an old man gazes at the moon.

8. Journey and a Box of Talismans

On September 16, 1819, the poet Issa attends a chrysanthemum-viewing
party in Shofuin's house where host and friends drink from tiny cups and
walk among chrysanthemums. In 1820, Issa's third son dies. In 1822,
his fourth son and beloved wife. His next two marriages, doomed, and in
1827, his house, burns to ashes.

Marking this year of my life
firecrackers, a paper lion
and a single cry
from a human throat:
I throw beans at demons!

CAMERA OBSCURA
—for Carol

A limb falls in the ice storm bending
the iron lawn table
like taffy

    (death will do this to us)

In the past I saw a pinhole of

                              light

as early as
December

on the
shortest
day

that began the lengthening   the opening   the warming

there was   the promise
there was   a hero
there was   spring

now a cataract clouds my eye in a world turned upside
down

the beast slays
the smallest vows lie broken

snow
       snows
             snows
                   snows

                         it goes

  dark

DANCE THERAPY

I face you, back against my wall.
You face me, back to your wall.

[music begins]

You call me forward. *Stop.*
You have the lead. I stop.
You size it up, the distance.

You call again. *Too close.*
Go back. I back off.
Safe now, you can see all of me—
no false steps, lunges, leaps in mid-air.

You hold your position.
I, mine.

My turn. I draw you out.
Come close, closer. Too close?
You stop there. Scared. Mad.
A backbend. A headstand. I'll do
anything to change the call.
Too late.

[music intensifies]

Forehead
to forehead, palms to palms.
Our feet stomp the beat.
Your chest a conga drum, my
fingers, castanets. Close enough
to kiss. You snarl your lip,
I bare my neck.

Time is up.

THAT ONE
(tanka sequence)

They are all
around you and they love
you so much
but there is one—That
One—watch out.

That One trips
you up, sends you spinning.
Foul mouth
pisses himself. Open
the outhouse door.

You can't stand it.
That One's raw anger.
Dragon breath.
Or is it you, hothead?
Empty the foul trash.

That One stalks.
taunts, spits. Hits
below the belt.
I get it. His fist
is my hot fear.

Dark One sulks.
Farts, sneers, ensnares.
Look out, he jeers.
Keep it to yourself.
You are only me.

I turn around.
That One—sick,
scrawny, scared.
Curl up near,
be Dark to my Light.

Now on walks
he rants and raves and I
say nothing.
It's cool. I
accept the Dark Me.

COUSINS
—for H.L.F.

My mother's cure for colic was to stop
my cries with karo syrup and a closed
door. Your faints—from a heart defect—
were *just you,* your mother said, *putting
on a good show.* Where we

come from, hope never sprang. Women
ruled, dragging us along on visits to sisters
and sisters-in-law who sparred with each
other and mocked the men they failed
to love. When all five

of our mothers' brothers came back
from WWII alive, our grandmother put
the *kibosh* on their Five-Blue-Star-Flag
and FDR's letter with one clipped
phrase: *Well, you know,*

she said, *only the good die young.*
Where we come from, dreams never
rose above the floorboards. Genius
was squashed with a black look.
Faces were slapped

for being beautiful. In those houses,
sisters were mothers, mothers were
sisters, and a father or uncle could
be your lover. Of all the cousins,
you and I

survive. We keep the family albums.
We trace the genealogy. We invest in
psychotherapy. In this photo of our
Catholic-immigrant clan, front row,
wriggling under your

mother's girth, you wave and smile
as if to say Look at me, I'm the cute one,
the friendly one, the funny one. And I
say, Look at me. I'm writing it all down
and giving the story away.

ANNIVERSARY

In kindergarten, you had kids
stick crayons up their noses
and walk around like walruses.
I was teacher's pet, sang Mass
with nuns, made sacrifices.
I had designs on the paperboy,
took his little red wagon; tried
to sleep with a boy on his mat
at naptime. Carla became
a Brownie, learned to draw
horses so you would marry her.
You made a finger trap from
your milk bottle wire with intent
to torture. Now you and I play
games: cat and mouse, push
'n pull, tit for tat. But flash back
to that first night when I refused
to let you get away. We touched,
we fit, we knew, and you said
you'd found *the One*. And on
this spring day, remember how
we, our long hair cut short, walked
into our life together. Without father,
mother, scripture, or God, we said
we'd take, we'd have, we'd do.
And we did, gladly, all these years.

HER GARDEN

It's so beautiful, she said
when I brought her the first
narcissus, the first magnolia
bloom. *It's so beautiful.*
She, unable to plant or weed,
let me lift her from the wheelchair
to the ground, where I handed
her a spadeful of dirt she smelled,
then threw down for me to tamp.
Later, she grew anxious,
demanding. Plant the bulbs.
Divide the Solomon's Seal.
Transplant the roses! I carted
St. Francis home for the rock
garden. My brother bought her
two flowering pears. His daughter
and I planted chrysanthemums.
His wife pruned the peonies.
It was too much for us, too
much for her. As they lifted her
off to the hospital, an October
chorus of yellow crocuses made
their appearance. At last her
garden was prepared. Coreopsis,
marigold, zinnia, gloriosa, we
laid them all in her bed.
All went with her into the fire.

LAST PEACH

Mm-Mm, Margo, he'd say, *you should have
seen the goodies—rice pudding, chocolate
bread, apple fritters and homemade ice cream,*

yum-yumming in my face and when he got to
shoofly pie, a pinch drove home the ecstasy,
along with a big *Ooooo-Ooooey!* Food was

better than sex for my Dad. He was a mama's
boy whose wife wouldn't coddle him. His father
drank but Dad wouldn't touch a drop. Instead,

he turned to Jesus, Hershey's kisses and
root beer. We came together late in life;
I didn't know he had what I had—a lust

for sticky buns, doughnuts, caramel fudge
and whoopee pies to make up for the sweetness
that was missing. At Dad's family reunions,

we made up for lost time. After he led prayers,
shared the news, slipped in a long-winded story
or two; after everyone shouted, *Enough, Woody,*

that's enough!, we two sat and chowed down
Amish potato salad, pork and sauerkraut, red
beet eggs, snickerdoodles, and slice after slice

of shoofly. I was with him for his last meal
at the nursing home when she wouldn't wheel
him into the bathroom to throw it all up, but I

did; and I sat on his narrow bed and held out
a perfect summer peach, ripe, luscious, the color
of sunset. We gazed at it for minutes; he patted

his sunken belly under the white gown, gave a sorry
look and said, *Can't do it, Margo.* I put the peach
in my pocket. We both let out a big sigh, and cried.

BARDO

...bardo is a... juncture when the possibility of liberation,
or enlightenment, is heightened. —The Tibetan Book of Living & Dying

You answer your cell.
Not at home, where are you?

I'm in Arizona, in a room,
surrounded by hummingbirds.

I hear you smiling. A ruby-throated
zips by, buzzing, humming.

In Virginia, crows caw, cricket
sounds cease, signaling the end.

In Texas she's dying. Will
you help me send Reiki?

I've tried to cup her in my hand,
visualize her spirit, and chant,

"Go out the top so you won't
have to come back again!"

But I don't know the distant healing
symbol. Will you show me?

You don't need it. Focus on
your love and intent.

I pray for the Buddha in me to
reach out to the Buddha in her.

But how can I—can she—love
a self swarming with cells that

don't know how to die?
We are all dying. Eagle, fox,

manatee, primrose, plover.
Lady cat's tumor burst, she stayed

a while, eye to my eye, then twice
a gentle cough, a burst of breath,

legs swimming and goodbye.
In this between time, I've fallen

into a nest of demons, caved
in to the illusion that horns and

howling, grasping hands are real.
But you—you—are in a room,

surrounded by hummingbirds.
And inside the clamor, under

the web of tears, in the turning
of flesh to dust, I'm saved

by a tiny heartbeat, a flame
of iridescent red and

emerald green; standstill
wings whirring.

SURRENDER

At eight
spring
knocked
me out
bowled me
over gob-
smacked
me   every
tree—redbud
cherry, plum
peach
—a shock
of color
a blast
of scent
lifting
me
up

At sixteen
I lay with
a boy
naked
in my
mother's
bed   gold
filtering
through half-
closed blinds
no need for
sex, every-
thing said
in a look
a hunger
an in-
drawn
breath

At sixty-
four I
climb
a green
over-
look
throw
myself
down
under a
wanton
magnolia
awake
all
night
stunned
by
stars

THANKS to the many poets who have shared and workshopped poetry with me, especially the Winding River Writers—Heather Davis, Kristin Zimet, and Kira Tomlin, who helped bring this book to fruition; to Laura Levesque who turned me on to NaPoWriMo and the awesome Autumn Sky Poetry poets; to Cathy McArthur and Woodside-on-the-Move where we heard and were heard by the day's best poets; and to MaryAnne Weinstein and Marybeth Lareau for their love, collaborations, and daily writing support and inspiration.

SPECIAL THANKS to my Hopewell Centre Meeting Friends (Quakers) who nurture my gifts (and buy my books), especially Robyn Harris who aided me and cheered me on through the publishing process, and Martha Hanley who is always there for me.

And finally, a VERY SPECIAL THANKS to my mentor, Colette Inez, for calling me to be a "sister" in poetry; to Manny Shapiro who helped put the broken pieces back together; to Carol Goode for her unconditional love; and to my husband Peter, who heard me read and said, "my ears, your voice — we danced!"

MAGGIE (MARGARET) STETLER is a survivor of childhood trauma, and has lived with chronic anxiety and depression all her life. Two things saved her: thirty-plus years of intense psychoanalysis and a lifetime of writing poetry.

Although this is Maggie's first full-length poetry collection at the age of 72, she has been published widely since the '70s, including in the iconic *Telephone* (St. Mark's Poetry Project), *Kosmos*, *The Small Pond Magazine of Literature*, and *WomanChild*. A chapbook, *The Naming of the Soul*, was published in 1980 (Four Zoas/Night House), and a photo/poem chapbook, *The Chain*, and *11 Broadsides: Poems & Pictures* were self-published.

Maggie has read at Manhattan's Donnell Library, Queens College, Provincetown Playhouse, and other venues in New York City, where she lived and worked until 2002. Her poems, collages and drawings have hung in galleries in NYC's Soho and City Island, and at the Shenandoah Arts Council (ShenArts) in Virginia.

Her work is currently in the *Buddhist Poetry Review*, *The Sow's Ear Poetry Review*, *Friends Journal*, *Undertow Tanka*, *Snapdragon: A Journal of Art and Healing*, *Autumn Sky Poetry Daily*, and in the anthologies, *Gathered: Contemporary Quaker Poets* (Sundress) and *Waves: A Confluence of Women's Voices* (AROHO). She was a finalist in the *Pearl* Poetry Contest.

Maggie holds a BA in English from Douglass College, Rutgers University. In Winchester, VA, where she now resides, she leads a workshop, "Freeing the Creative Artist Within You;" is a frequent Guest Poet at the city's public schools and the Shenandoah Valley Discovery Museum; and she has adjudicated for The Poetry Society of Virginia's student contests and for Poetry Out Loud. She is a member of the Winding River Writers and Shenandoah Poetry Alliance.

Maggie lives with her artist husband, Peter Stetler (and yes, three cats). She substitute teaches and loves working with students with special needs. Maggie is an advocate for the mentally ill and abused, and she champions the creative arts as a means to heal and transform broken lives.

www.ingramcontent.com/pod-product-compliance
Lightning Source LLC
Chambersburg PA
CBHW021158090426
42740CB00008B/1141